Keep Calm
and
Carry On

*A handbook to choose your
emotions and change your attitude*

Jonathan Forrest and Andrew Hughes-Hallett

The original Keep Calm and Carry On poster was created by the British government in 1939 as part of a series of inspirational posters designed to help the people of Britain stay positive during a time of crisis.

Millions of copies of this poster were printed but never displayed and the poster and its message were forgotten until a copy was discovered in a box of books bought at auction by a bookseller in 2000 who subsequently displayed the poster in his shop. Following coverage in a national newspaper, copies of the poster were sold and its message replicated on to other goods.

Whilst many people worldwide have been inspired by the message of Keep Calm and Carry On, there has never been any guidance on HOW to Keep Calm and Carry On - until now...

"Keep Calm and Carry On - A handbook to choose your emotions and change your attitude" is an original copyright work of which the authors are Messrs. Jonathan Forrest and Andrew Hughes-Hallett.

© Forrest and Hughes-Hallett 2010.

ISBN: 978-1-4461-9183-5

Each of the authors hereby separately asserts his right to be identified as author of this work in accordance with the Copyright, Design and Patents Act 1988.

The Authors

Jonathan Forrest is a leadership development consultant and executive coach working with organisations across the globe. Originally training as an opera singer, but deciding against a career in professional singing, he has held various leadership positions at global organisations. His last major corporate role was as Vice President at Goldman Sachs where he worked on designing and delivering Goldman's pioneering in-house global leadership programme. He now runs his own leadership development consultancy and executive coaching practice.

Andrew Hughes-Hallett is a business development consultant working with corporations throughout Europe and the Middle East. Having pioneered the introduction of world renowned business speakers to Europe in the early nineties, he established his own management development consultancy in 1995. Through its innovative and energetic approach, the company acquired successful and long term relationships with dozens of FTSE 100 companies, whilst expanding a network of offices across EMEA. In 2005 as Executive Chairman, he led the company to a merger to create a global consultancy before negotiating his exit from the business in 2006. He now advises on leadership and strategy.

Chapter 1

Understanding your Emotion and Attitudes

The sound that pierced the silence made Ferdinand Jones' heart race and, for a second, he did not know where he was. Suddenly, his brain kicked into gear and it all made sense. Ferdi reached out and turned off the alarm. The illuminated digits on his clock radio told him it was 4.30 am. Time to get up.

Ferdi had been rising at 4.30 am for as long as he could remember but on winter mornings like this one, getting out of bed was not easy. Ferdi glanced at the shape in bed next to him. His wife Marina was laying on her back with the duvet tucked up to her chin. He leaned over and carefully pulled out the plugs that were stuffed into her ears. Marina wore earplugs every night so that Ferdi's alarm did not wake her, but they had to be removed or she would sleep through her own wake-up call at 7.30 am. Ferdi joked that Marina could sleep for England and, without her alarm, she would still be snoozing at lunchtime. Thankfully, Ferdi was so used to this early morning ritual that Marina never heard or felt a thing and snored away gently for three more hours. Three glorious hours! Ferdi sank back into his pillow and felt the same pang of jealousy as he did every working day. His feelings of jealousy passed in an instant as Ferdi pushed the negative thoughts out of his mind and reminded himself why he got up at this time regardless of the weather or any of the many other reasons he could find to stay in bed. If Ferdi did not get out of bed and go to work, he would not earn any money and, if he did not earn any money, his life would not be the same.

Earning a living was for Ferdi about much more than simply paying the mortgage, covering the family's day-to-day expenses and the occasional holiday in the Mediterranean.

It made him who he was and it gave him his sense of self and, as much as he loved his family and friends, nothing would keep him away from it.

He glanced at the clock again. 4.40 am. Now he really did have to make a move. It was time to leave the sanctuary of his warm bed and venture out into the world; work was waiting. He slipped out from under the duvet and gave Marina a kiss on the cheek. As Ferdi slowly made his way to the bathroom the cold air made him shiver. If the weather stayed like this, he thought to himself, he would have to change the timer on the heating. Although Ferdi arose at 4.30 am the heating was set to come on at 6.30 am, ensuring the house was warm when Marina finally stirred. He was up and out of the house within 30 minutes and had always maintained that there was no need to heat the entire building for his quick ablutions but, if this cold snap continued, he might just change his mind.

After a quick shower and piping hot cup of tea, Ferdi was ready to face whatever the city threw his way. At 5.12 am precisely, he closed the front door behind him and headed for the car. As he turned the key in the ignition, Ferdi's working day began and for the next fifteen hours, his cab would be his world. Ever the optimist, Ferdi turned on the 'Taxi' light that signified he was for hire, and he was on his way.

Ferdi's closest friends Chris and Joe could not understand why he started work this early and Marina was convinced he would earn more on the night shift, but he loved early mornings on London's roads. The traffic was light, the air was crisp and, if he timed it right, he could be in the heart of the city just as the sun began to rise over the river. It was a sight he would never tire of and it made him feel glad to be alive.

Outside the taxi, it was freezing and a heavy frost covered the ground.

Ferdi glanced up and noticed that the dark sky had an eerie glow; it looked as though snow might fall before too long. Most people disliked the cold but not Ferdi, he had a different way of looking at things. Ferdi tried not to become overwhelmed by the things in his life that he could not change. He realised that the weather was completely out of his control so instead he focused his energies on the things he could affect such as his emotions and his attitude.

Ferdi had learned to take back the control of his emotions and therefore his life, the hard way. He had spent more time than he cared to think about feeling miserable and believing that the world had it in for him. Ferdi's life changed dramatically when he learnt to look for the positive rather than negative side to any situation.

The experts call it re-framing, but to Ferdi it was about taking a moment to look at a situation in a different way. Like most people, Ferdi's brain was wired to seek the negative rather than positive aspects of his life, something he had always assumed was simply down to his personality. While negativity is a natural human instinct, Ferdi now knew that with a concentrated effort, it could be changed. He was determined never to go back to his old dark days.

So Ferdi was not going to moan about the weather, instead he turned the heater up in the cab, smiled and reminded himself that cold days were always good for business. On days like today, people in the outskirts of the city wanted cabs. They would start out with good intentions and walk to the bus stop on their way to work but, unless one came along quickly, anyone feeling flush would hail a passing taxi.

Once the rush hour started, Ferdi would drive slowly past bus stops looking warm and comfortable. It would not take long before a hand shot up into the air and someone shouted, 'Taxi!' Usually the young, single, professionals hailed him from bus stops. They liked clothes that looked good although did not keep out the cold and they had the disposable income to spend on

impulsively hailed cabs. On days like today, Ferdi looked out for these overly fashion-conscious young people and he would happily take them to work in his warm taxi with comfort and style.

Ferdi's first stop of the morning was at the Blue Bell Cafe. It was an overly fragrant name for what was in reality a grubby greasy spoon with an interior stuck firmly in 1975. Ferdi stopped outside and tooted his horn. Bella came to the door and called out, 'Usual, Ferd?'

Ferdi had come here for breakfast every working day, only missing it on the rare occasions that he got a fare between leaving home and reaching Bella's. Bella knew his tastes well.

Today, as every day, 'the usual' was exactly what he wanted. Ferdi's guilty pleasure was a bacon roll with extra fried onions, grilled cheese and ketchup washed down with a mug of steaming-hot tea. No one made tea quite like Bella. She made a huge pot first thing in the morning and kept adding tea bags and hot water throughout the day. Ferdi was convinced that if he came back just before closing, the tea would be so strong you could strip wood with it.

As he watched Bella through the cafe's window, the voice of his GP, Doctor Juttla, ran through his head. Every time he saw her, regardless of his reason for visiting the surgery, she said the same thing, 'Ferdinand, you have to lose some weight. You must cut down on all these fatty foods and start exercising regularly.' She'd been trying to get Ferdi to diet and take up exercise for years and Ferdi knew that his job, which basically involved sitting down for fifteen hours a day, wasn't exactly healthy. Ferdi thought of a healthy diet and exercise as a sacrifice and a chore but he was working hard to alter this view. If he found the right exercise, it would be rewarding and possibly even fun and cutting out fatty foods was not a sacrifice if he found tasty options to replace them. Yes, he thought, I must try harder. Ferdi smiled to himself and decided that this should be his last fried breakfast for a while and he would definitely go to the gym after his shift today, definitely.

Bella shuffled out of the door and handed Ferdi the brown paper bag containing his breakfast, 'There you are Ferdi,' she said and added "cold enough for you?" as she pulled her cardigan around her more tightly. Bella did not wait for an answer and quickly headed back to the warmth of the cafe. 'Thanks Bella', Ferdi said and then called after her, 'look on the bright-side; this weather could be great for the cafe; put some huge bowls of hot soup on the menu and customers will be queuing out of the door.' With that, Ferdi turned his attention to breakfast and muttered, 'Sorry Doc,' quietly under his breath as he savoured the first delicious bite.

Ferdi sat back in his cab and enjoyed a few minutes of quiet reflection. Every morning, over his tea and bacon roll, he liked to list some of the things that were good about his life. The little day-to-day things that most people forgot about, like the freedom of being his own boss and deciding when and where he would work, watching football on Saturday afternoons, even breakfast at Bella's. Taking the time to appreciate what is good in his life enabled Ferdi to start each day feeling good about himself and his work. It helped to remind him why he did what he did and set him up for his shift in much the same way as his hearty breakfast.

It was this positive state of mind that helped Ferdi through the day. Driving a cab is not easy, especially in a city like London where you never know quite what is going to happen next. On his first day as a cabby, Ferdi had learnt there was much more to the job than simply taking people from A to B. A London Taxi driver is part tour guide, part therapist and part, Ferdi liked to think, super-hero. Getting people to where they want to go, when they want to be there and doing it with a smile requires a special type of person.

Luckily for his passengers, Ferdi has an ethos that he lives by and it is one he likes to share. Whatever happens Ferdi knows the best thing to do is

simply keep calm and carry on.

Although it was never actually used, Keep Calm & Carry On was a poster created during WWII by the British government to help morale. Ferdi had been introduced to the motto during his own terrible time and now has a Keep Calm & Carry On postcard attached to the taxi's dashboard as a constant reminder.

As Ferdi pulled away from the Blue Bell, he glanced at the card and smiled. Who would have thought that such a simple statement would have such a dramatic effect on his life?

To Ferdi 'keep calm' meant being able to choose his emotion. He could choose to be angry, depressed or frustrated or he could think differently and instead opt for happy, delighted or curious. He could decide to panic or remain calm. In an ideal world, there would be no other cabs except Ferdi's and he would always be busy; there would be no traffic jams to hold him up or disgruntled customers to complain about their fares. But life isn't like that, so instead Ferdi opted to look at situations differently, to reframe his thoughts; after all, there's always more than one way to look at things and choosing the positive option makes life so much more enjoyable.

"How do I manage to be this positive so early in the morning? The human brain is naturally wired to highlight negativity but, by changing the way it works, anybody can maintain a positive state of mind. Here is how I do it."

• *Do not allow yourself to become overwhelmed by the things you cannot change like the weather or other people's behaviour. Focus instead on what you can affect, like your emotions, thoughts and actions.*

• *As soon as you become aware of a negative thought entering your head or feelings of stress or anxiety altering your mindset, actively choose to revert to a more positive and resourceful state. After all, why would anyone want to feel angry or frustrated when they could feel happy or curious?*

• *Do this by looking at the situation in a different way – rather than simply following your first and instant reaction. Ask yourself why a person might have behaved in this way or why the situation has caused you to react so negatively.*

• *Often taking just a few moments to understand the situation and why you are feeling or behaving in a negative way will be enough to move you out of it.*

• *If all else fails and the situation is still getting you down, remind yourself of all the positives in your life, the little things that we often take for granted, but actually make our days complete.*

Chapter 2

Keep Calm

Had he been a betting man, Ferdi would have put money on his first customer being an office worker heading to the financial district of the city. He could not have been more wrong. The woman standing at the side of the road, waving her arm at him, was wearing a grey winter coat with a fur-trimmed hood - nothing unusual in that, you might think, but underneath she had on what looked like a pair of pink fleece pyjamas covered in big brown spots and on her feet were a matching pair of slippers.

As it was still early, Ferdi's first thought was that she might be sleepwalking so he pulled over a few feet in front of her, just in case she stepped out into the road. The woman ran up to the cab and got in. Ferdi turned to talk to her and noticed she was crying.

'Drive towards the park, please, but slowly,' she sobbed, as she took the tissue she was twisting in her hands and used it to wipe her eyes.

'Is everything okay, love?' Ferdi asked kindly as he pulled away from the kerb. He hated to see people upset and wondered if he could do anything to help his passenger.

'No, it is not,' she sobbed quietly, 'but I will be okay when we get to the park. Oh, and slow down please. I need you to drive as slowly as possible.' That is unusual, thought Ferdi as he slowed down to twenty miles an hour. He was more used to his fares wanting to get where they are going as quickly as possible.

'Are we going to the park, or stopping somewhere on the way?' he asked in curiosity, wondering why his passenger was wearing pyjamas and slippers on what was probably the coldest day of the year. There had to be a logical explanation, he thought; perhaps there was a sponsored walk at the park and she was running late.

'Head for the park first and then I'll decide from there,' she replied and sat looking forlornly out of the window.

Ferdi did as he was asked and took the quickest route to the park. He did not want to distress his passenger any more than she already was. Ferdi glanced at the rear-view mirror, the woman seemed to have stopped crying but still looked very unhappy.

As soon as they reached the park, his passenger went to open her door and Ferdi assumed she had reached her destination.

'That's £4.60 plea...' Ferdi did not get to finish his sentence.

'No, no, I need you to wait, we haven't finished yet,' she exclaimed, 'I just want to look around here for a minute, then I'll need you to either take me home or drive around for a little longer.'

Involuntary alarm bells went off in Ferdi's head; his immediate reaction was to think that everything was wrong about this fare and that he should cut his losses and go. But Ferdi was determined that negativity wouldn't take over his emotions so early in the day and, what's more, his conscience would not allow him to leave a woman wearing pyjamas alone in the park; it was still dark. He glanced at his Keep Calm & Carry On postcard, took a deep breath and decided that he would treat the woman with kindness and the situation with curiosity. After all, there had to be a good reason why she was behaving this way and he would find out and do all he could to help.

His passenger ran up to the park entrance and shouted, 'Daisy. Daisy, where are you? Daisy!' She is looking for someone, thought Ferdi, which would explain her erratic behaviour. He waited in the cab to see what would happen next and watched events unfold with interest.

The woman ran further along the path and called out again, 'Daisy, please come back! Mummy's here. Daisy, where are you, darling?!' Ferdi felt the blood drain from his face; she had lost her child. He switched off the engine and called out of his window, 'Oh no, why didn't you say what was wrong? I will help you look for Daisy.' Ferdi got out of the cab and, walking carefully over the frost-covered pavement, went over to where she was standing.

'How old is Daisy?' Ferdi asked as he made his way towards the woman, hoping the child would be old enough to safely cross the busy roads that ran between where he had picked up her mum and the park.

'She's six and a half,' the woman replied. Ferdi's heart sank. It was a long way for such a young girl to come by herself and he hoped that she was okay and that they would find her here. He did not want to upset his passenger further and did not mention his concerns to her.

Ferdi was quite breathless from the exertion of getting out of his cab and making his way across the pavement, so he leaned against the park gates to get his breath back. Ferdi's eyes were watering from the cold but pure adrenalin was enough to keep his body warm.

'Thank you! Thank you so much for offering to help,' she said gratefully and gave Ferdi a hug. ' But, are you okay?'

I must look a sorry state thought Ferdi, but he smiled and said, 'I just needed to catch my breath but I am fine. Now, let us look for Daisy. When did you last see her?'

'She must have slipped out when I was talking to the postman, I did not realise she was gone for a good 10 minutes. She could be anywhere and I'm going out of my mind with worry.'

'Have you called the police?' Ferdi asked, hoping they were out looking for Daisy as well. He had heard on the news that the first two hours were crucial in finding lost children.

'No, I wanted to see if I could find her first,' she replied and burst into tears again. Ferdi gave her a fresh tissue from his pocket as her own was in pieces.

'Don't cry,' Ferdi added gently. I will call her; I can shout much louder than you. 'Daisy! Daisy! Mummy's here. Daisy,' he yelled as loudly as he could, then added in a quieter and rather more controlled tone, 'You don't know me ,but I'm helping Mummy look for you, don't be frightened.' They both looked around hopefully and called out a few more times, but the park was deserted and there was no sign of anyone, let alone Daisy.

'Try not to worry too much, ' Ferdi sighed, 'I'm sure she will be okay and if we don't find her, the police will.' The woman nodded sadly.

'Was she wearing a coat? It is freezing out here today,' asked Ferdi.

'Of course! I don't get her coat clipped in the winter. It is very thick and keeps her nice and warm. Thank goodness Westies are from Scotland,' she said, 'they're used to the cold.'

'Westies! What do you mean?'

'West Highland Terriers, you know those cute little dogs with lovely shaggy fur. Daisy's coat is white,' she added, hugging herself as she spoke, oblivious to the look of confusion on Ferdi's face. As he realised what was going on, his confusion turned to annoyance. 'A dog!' Ferdi said harshly. The woman looked puzzled by his reaction and said, 'Sorry, I don't understand.'

'You mean to tell me that after all this worry and stress, we are only looking for a dog?' Ferdi continued. He could not believe what he was hearing; he had been at his wits end with worry over a missing dog.

'She is not 'only' a dog, she is my dog and she means everything to me. How could you say something so heartless?' she replied, tears welling up in her eyes once again.

Ferdi felt terrible for reacting so thoughtlessly and upsetting his passenger all over again. His outburst, he realised, had nothing to do with the passenger or her dog and everything to do with his ego. He felt foolish for not finding out exactly who or what they were looking for, and for assuming - wrongly - that he was looking for a person. Thank goodness he had not called the police.

The woman had started to sob loudly again, so Ferdi apologised as he gently led her back to the cab. 'I'm really sorry,' he said. 'I should not have spoken to you like that and I do understand that you must be very worried, it's just that I thought we were looking for your child.'

'But I don't have any children.'

'Okay, but I didn't know that…' Ferdi decided against trying to explain and instead asked, 'Can you think of anywhere else she might have gone?'

'Not really, I had already looked around the streets near my house before I hailed you, the park was my last hope.'

'Has Daisy got any doggie friends she might have gone to visit?'

'Not really,' the woman replied earnestly, 'she usually meets her friends at the park. That is why I came here. Can we just drive around for a little longer? We might spot her wandering about.'

'Of course,' he smiled, 'whatever you want, you're the boss'.

The early morning rush to work had begun and the roads were filling up with traffic. Ferdi's cab was driving at just fifteen miles an hour and therefore causing frustration to the other road users.

A double-decker bus driver blasted his horn and gesticulated wildly to show his displeasure and several cars flashed their headlights to try and get him to speed up but Ferdi did his best to ignore them all and focused instead on scanning the streets for missing Daisy. Ferdi wished he could explain to the other road users why he was driving as slowly as he was, they might calm down if they realised what was going on. He understood why they were getting angry but knew it was not necessary; road rage would not solve anything. Perhaps his Keep Calm & Carry On postcard should become mandatory for all road users. Ferdi smiled at the thought; maybe he should get in contact with Transport for London and suggest it.

Ten minutes later, he was still driving around and there was no sign of Daisy. 'Do you think it's worth going home to see if Daisy has headed back there?', Ferdi suggested. 'It's the place she knows and loves best and she'd probably expect you to be there.'

'I guess so,' she sighed, 'I suppose there's little point in driving up and down the streets all morning.'

'Once you're at home you can call the police and the RSPCA to see if she's been handed in.' Ferdi said.

'You're right. Thank you! It's a good job one of us is thinking straight.'

'My motto in life is 'keep calm and carry on.' I find that if I can do that, everything usually works out okay in the end.'

'Keeping calm is easier said than done when something like this happens,' she said sadly as she wiped her eyes and continued to look out of the window.

'It makes sense though,' replied Ferdi. 'When I panic I end up using all my energy on feeling stressed and don't actually do anything useful about the situation.' His passenger nodded in agreement, so Ferdi added, 'I know it sounds daft but I find deep-breathing helps too.' Ferdi knew this was true, short, shallow breaths deprive the blood supply of oxygen, which adds to feelings of anxiety, while deep breathing calms and relaxes the body.

'Deep breathing?' Daisy's owner sounded confused.

'I might not look like a deep-breather,' Ferdi laughed, 'but if a bloke like me can do it anyone can'.

His passenger smiled for the first time, so Ferdi continued. 'Smiling really helps too as it changes your facial expression which automatically alters your mindset. Try it next time you're feeling low; a smile has an instantaneous positive effect.'

'I'll try to keep smiling then,' she replied, sounding happier than she had done all morning. 'Now tell me about this deep breathing.'

'Okay.' Ferdi replied, 'What you do is, breathe in slowly through your nose to fill your lungs and then let the air out again through your mouth.' Ferdi demonstrated, then added, 'To do it properly you have to focus on your breathing and if you start to focus on your breathing you stop focussing on whatever it is that is causing you to worry. I find it calms me right down and clears my head. Then I can work out what to do for the best.'

'Like go and see if Daisy has returned home? You're right, it does make sense.'

'It takes practice but you will get there in the end. Like I said; if a cabby like me can do it! Now, what's your address?'

'125 Phoenix Road, please.' Ferdi turned the taxi around and headed back to Phoenix Road. As they were travelling against the traffic, the ride took less than five minutes. For the length of the journey, the woman sat in the back of the cab with her eyes closed and practised her deep breathing. Ferdi smiled to himself, he was amazed how few people realised that they are the ones in control of their emotions and therefore how they feel at any given

moment. All it takes is a few simple techniques, conscious thought and a desire to want to change.

By the time I get her home, he thought, she will be in a much better frame of mind and that is bound to help her find her dog. He closed the glass partition between himself and his passenger and left her to her breathing.

'Here we are,' said Ferdi quietly as they pulled up outside her house. 'Do you feel any calmer?'

'Do you know what; I think I do,' she sounded surprised, 'and, I've just remembered, I went into the garage this morning. Perhaps Daisy followed me in there. If not, she has a tag with her address and phone number on. I know that someone will find her and either call me or hand her in to the RSPCA.' 'I'm sure you are right,' smiled Ferdi as his passenger got out of the cab, 'good luck. Oh, and get some clothes on, before you catch a cold!'

Ferdi watched as his passenger went to her garage and opened the door. A bundle of white fur ran out and jumped up at the woman's legs. Case solved.

A £17 fare and some useful cabby advice dispensed. Ferdi loved this job. Now, he thought, where is the nearest bus stop?

FERDI'S THOUGHTS

"If you start to focus on your breathing you stop focussing on whatever it is that is causing you to worry."

"Do I ever get upset or frustrated? Of course I do, I am only human after all. However, in most situations, frustration will not get you anywhere and you will achieve much more in a calm, resourceful state. Here are some of my favourite tricks for keeping calm and clear thinking."

Deep Breathing

Take a few deep breaths to help clear your mind and release tension from your body. Usually, during times of anxiety, we tend to breathe using short, shallow breaths that limit our oxygen intake and actually heighten the feelings of stress. Here's how to breathe properly:

- *Breathe in slowly through your nose. If you are breathing deeply, your stomach will extend (shallow breathing causes the stomach to move in, rather than out).*

- *Hold your breath for a count of two, and then slowly exhale through your mouth. As you do this, your stomach will move inwards.*

- *Repeat this two or three times or until you feel calm.*

Facial Expressions

Smile! It sounds too simple, but the fastest way to feel happier is to smile.

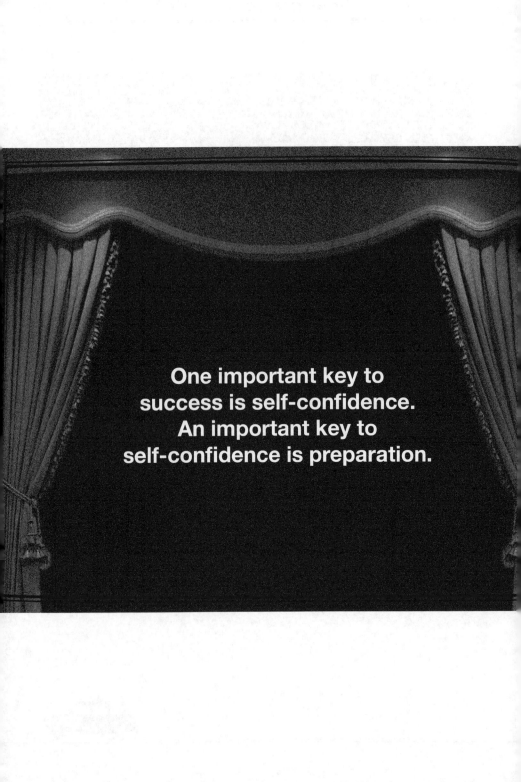

One important key to success is self-confidence. An important key to self-confidence is preparation.

Chapter 3

Choose your emotions - Angry or Calm?

Ferdi's morning was going well. A young woman wearing trainers and a suit had hailed him near Harrow Road and Ferdi guessed that she had intended to walk to work, but the cold had forced a change of mind. She asked to be dropped off at Baker Street, pulled a laptop computer out of her bag, and began tapping away. Her only comment to Ferdi was to ask if he was wi-fi enabled.

'Sorry,' he replied, 'I haven't got wi-fi but I have got a heater and comfortable seats.' His passenger laughed and said, 'That's good enough for me.'

From Baker Street he picked up a fare that had taken him to Piccadilly Circus. After that, he had driven people from hotels to office blocks and from office blocks to train stations. None of them had been jobs he could retire on, but it was good bread and butter work of the £10 to £20 variety.

Ferdi's next job had been pre-booked. He had to get from his last drop-off in Paddington to Kennington for 11 am Kennington is south of the river and Ferdi wanted to be sure he was on time, so at 10.30 am he switched off his 'Taxi' sign, grabbed a take-away coffee and a newspaper and headed south.

Twenty minutes after leaving Paddington, Ferdi pulled up outside number 65 Walden Road and tooted his horn. A man's face peered out from behind the blind and stuck up his thumb, to signify he was on his way out.

'I reckon I've just got time to read the back page of the paper,' Ferdi thought to himself, and settled down to the match reports from the previous night's games. He had just unfolded his newspaper when there was a tapping on the near-side window.

'I think this is my cab. The name is Johnson.'

'Sure is, hop in.' Ferdi refolded the paper and put it away. He hoped he would get a chance to read it before the headlines became yesterday's news.

The fare was in his early 20's, tall and slim with untidy brown hair that flopped over his pale face. He looked worried and started biting his nails almost as soon as he sat down.

'Cold enough for you?' The weather is always a good conversation starter and Ferdi felt it was his duty to take Mr. J's mind off his nails.

'Yeah! It is freezing,' was his only reply before starting on his nails again. I am going to have to cut to the chase, thought Ferdi.

'You off to an interview or have you got a vendetta against your nails?' he asked with a smile.

Mr. J smiled back, 'I always bite my nails when I'm stressed and I'm feeling very stressed today.'

'Biting your nails won't stop you feeling stressed, it'll just make your hands look like they've been through a mangle,' Ferdi laughed. 'Seriously though, mate, what is making you feel so anxious?'

'Just work stuff.'

'Work! What are you, a brain surgeon or something?'

Mr. J smiled, 'No, I'm an actor.'

'An actor, eh! I have had a few actors in the back. Would I have seen you in anything?' Ferdi, like most taxi drivers, loved to have a 'name' in the back of the cab and hoped this fare would be worth a few brownie points in the taxi rank queue or with Marina over dinner.

'Not unless you've been to any of my drama school productions.'

'Still learning your trade then?' asked Ferdi, disappointed that he was not the latest recruit to Eastenders or the next Doctor Who.

'I think I will always be learning, but I have just finished drama school. You're taking me to my first proper audition.'

'So that's why you're stressed, it all makes sense now.'

'Yep!' he replied while chewing viciously at the side of his index finger.

'Doesn't that hurt?' Ferdi could not help asking.

'A bit,' was all the reply he got. Ferdi changed the subject back to the audition.

'What part are you up for?'

'It is a TV job. If I get it, I'll be playing the teenage son in a sitcom.'

'Sounds good, you must be excited.' At that comment, Mr. J began attacking his thumbnail. Nerves are a terrible thing, thought Ferdi, and tried to put himself in Mr. J's position. He would probably be a jabbering wreck if it were he going to audition for his first big break. Ferdi remembered how he had felt when trying to pass The Knowledge; the world famous route test that London Taxi drivers have to pass in order get their badge and licence.

'Is the nail biting helping you get in character?

'No, I am just terrified. I really want this job and now I'm having doubts about my audition piece.'

'What are you doing?'

Mr. J put his head in his hands, 'I was going to do the prince's opening soliloquy from Hamlet; I had based it on David Tennant's portrayal at the RSC. But now I'm not so sure.'

'What aren't you sure about?' asked Ferdi.

'Shakespeare's a bit predictable and my flat-mate said my Scottish accent's dodgy.'

'Is the character you're auditioning for Scottish?' Ferdi asked, concerned about what the answer might be.

'No!' was his anguished reply.

'So why are you doing your audition in a Scottish accent?' Ferdi had to ask the obvious question.

'Because Tennant did the version of Hamlet that I've based it on.'

'Right!' said Ferdi, curious about the clarity of his passenger's thought process, 'I do not know much about auditions, but if they wanted to cast a Scottish actor they would not be auditioning you. Surely they want to cast a young English actor who can pass as a teenager and deliver a well-timed joke.'

'Oh my goodness, I've blown it.' Mr. J cried and put his head in his hands.

'Of course you haven't,' Ferdi told him. 'Could you deliver the same piece but in a different way?'

'No, it is too late. I can't rework Shakespeare.' With that, Mr. J went back to his nails and added, 'You might as well turn round and take me home now.'

'Why?' asked Ferdi. He was surprised that Mr. J would even consider missing what could be his big break.

'There's no point in putting myself through the humiliation.' Ferdi wanted to do something to help and looked at his Keep Calm & Carry On postcard for inspiration. 'I hope you don't mind me saying, but I think you're looking at this situation in a very negative way and trust me, negativity won't help you get this part.'

'I'm not negative, I'm a realist,' was Mr. J's reply.

'How about being a positive realist, it will make life a lot more enjoyable and I guarantee you'll be more successful,' said Ferdi with a smile.

'I was born a pessimist, I am afraid. Positivity does not come naturally to me at all,' laughed Mr. J.

'I don't believe that,' replied Ferdi. 'No one is a born pessimist and while positivity does not come naturally to most people it is something you can work at being.'

'Do not get me wrong,' said Mr. J, 'I do try to be positive but it does not last. My true miserable self is always lurking in the background. Anyway, we can't all be perky like you cab drivers.'

'Being "perky" isn't easy,' replied Ferdi. 'I have to work at it all the time, but I've discovered that while I don't have much control over most of the things that happen day to day, what I can affect is how I feel.'

'How so?'

'Well, I think that the first step in achieving a positive state of mind is to look at whatever you feel concerned about, differently.' Mr. J looked interested and had finally stopped biting his nails, so Ferdi continued. 'Instead of deciding that the audition will go badly, think about what you can do to ensure it goes well and that you get the part.'

'I don't understand what you mean.' replied Mr. J.

'Well,' said Ferdi, 'anything in life can be looked at in a number of different ways, but sadly most of us automatically opt for the most negative option. I will give you an example; you are walking down a quiet street and see a young lad running towards you. It is dark and a hooded jacket covers his head. What goes through your mind?'

'He's going to steal my phone.'

'It is natural for us to only consider negative outcomes and yet the chances that he is going to rob you are very small. He's probably running for the bus or knows his mum will go mad if he's late for dinner.'

'Okay, I'll try not to assume that everyone wearing a hoodie is going to rob me, but how will that help me with my audition?' asked a sceptical Mr. J.

'Forget not turning up, forget humiliating yourself. Look at the situation differently, decide what you can do to make the audition a success.'

'That's the problem,' cried Mr. J, despondently, 'I don't know what to do differently.'

'Let us think about something else for a few minutes,' suggested Ferdi. 'It might help your mind focus on what to do next. What's your favourite dish to cook?'

'Er, spaghetti bolognese,' answered his passenger, not sure why the discussion had suddenly turned to food.

'Tell me how to make it, step by step,' said Ferdi, 'and don't leave anything out.' A bemused Mr. J went through his recipe for spaghetti. When he finished, Ferdi said, 'If you get the job you can cook that for me. Now, what can you do to have a role-winning audition?'

'Perhaps I should do a different piece,' Mr. J answered hopefully. I think he's got it, thought Ferdi. It was a technique he often found himself using. Whenever he was not sure of what to do for the best or wanted to change his mood, he would think about or do something completely different, even if it was just for a moment or two.

'That's a good place to start, any ideas as to what?' asked Ferdi.

'I did a production at drama school where I played a teenage tear-away. That would work,' he said sounding positive for the first time.

'Sounds perfect, can you remember the dialogue?'

'I'm not sure, it was about a year ago.'

'Why don't you run through it now and if you forget anything, improvise.'

'How long until we get to Soho?' asked Mr. J.

'Ten minutes, give or take a bit.'

'I'd better get to it then.'

Ferdi turned off his radio so that he could listen to Mr. J's rehearsal in the background and still focus on his driving. He had just turned into Shaftesbury Avenue when he saw a young man in a wheelchair struggling to get from the road onto the pavement. A car had parked in front of the dipped section of pavement, which meant the deep kerb was his only route off of the congested road. Ferdi was sitting in a row of traffic two cars away from the man and he had enough experience of disability to know that he would never make it on to the pavement without help. Shaftesbury Avenue was full of pedestrians making their way to Soho or Chinatown and yet no one stopped to help the man who was now leaning back so far in an attempt to lift his front wheels onto the pavement, that he looked in serious danger of falling out of his chair.

Ferdi was shocked that none of the passers-by were helping. He could feel his anger rising and, unable to contain himself any longer, opened his window and shouted at the top of his voice, 'Can't you people see that man needs help? One of you help him get his wheelchair out of the road. Now!' The forceful tone of Ferdi's voice brought the crowd to their senses and a teenage boy stopped and pulled the man and his wheelchair backwards up on to the kerb.

'Sometimes I wonder if disabled people are invisible,' Ferdi muttered to himself as he closed his window and edged the taxi forward, 'and the driver who parked on the crossing deserves more than a parking ticket.'
'Are you alright?' asked a startled Mr. J, who had finished his run-through just before Ferdi had started shouting. His driver had been an oasis of calm until that point and he was surprised at this dramatic change in his temperament.

Ferdi explained what had happened, 'Sorry about that, but that disabled man in a wheelchair was trapped in the road and no-one was bothering to help him. I'd have preferred not to lose my temper and shout out of the window, but sometimes even anger has its place.'

'Yes, I suppose it does; well done for getting someone to help.' replied Mr. J. 'Most people wouldn't have bothered.'

'I wish I could have got out and helped him myself,' added Ferdi quietly to himself.

Ferdi had used his anger to get the results he needed from the people on the pavement but now he knew he had to take his state of mind back to a more resourceful one. If he did not focus on doing it now, it would be all too easy to end up in a bad mood for the rest of the day. Ferdi's heart was beating fast from his body going into the instinctive 'fight or flight' reaction that comes with stress. He took three deep breaths to slow it down and felt himself growing calmer almost straight away. Next, he wanted to take his mind away from the feelings of anger by focusing on something else. I know, he thought to himself, I will see if I can remember the names of the English 1966 World Cup winning team. No, he thought, that is too easy; I will name the entire squad. Even the idea made him smile; Ferdi loved a football challenge.

'Springett, Bonetti, Armfield, Eastham, Hunt, Cohen, Stiles, Moore…'

'Sorry, didn't quite catch that,' said Mr. J, who thought Ferdi was speaking to him.

'I was talking to myself; reciting the 1966 world cup squad.'

'Okay, dare I ask why?' asked a bemused Mr. J.

'Seeing the disabled man struggle without any help made me really angry, but I don't want to remain in that resentful mood for the rest of the day,' Ferdi explained. 'So to take my mind away from what happened, I'm focusing on something else, the 1966 World Cup winning squad.'

'Where did you learn all this?' asked Mr. J, 'and I don't mean the squad, I mean all this keeping calm, mind-focusing stuff?'

'That's a long story,' smiled Ferdi, 'I'll tell you, when you cook me that spaghetti bolognese.'

'You've got a deal,' said Mr. J.

A few moments later, they arrived and Mr. J headed into the audition.

'Good luck,' called Ferdi, 'Although I don't think you'll need it; your audition piece sounded great. But, whatever happens, remember that you can choose your emotions and your state of mind.' Mr. J waved and walked away from the cab with a smile on his face. He will do fine, Ferdi thought to himself, and smiled as he flicked on his 'Taxi' sign. He drove off looking for his next fare.

"How about being a positive realist - it will make life a lot more enjoyable and I guarantee you'll be more successful."

"Can I ever justify being angry? It is not a state I choose lightly, but there are situations when it can be helpful. The important thing is not to stay angry for any longer than absolutely necessary"

- *There may be occasions where even a normally unresourceful emotion such as anger is the most appropriate or necessary emotion. For example, in an emergency or where you have tried everything else.*

- *Once the situation has passed, use focused thought to get your brain back to a more resourceful and useful state.*

- *Focussed thought kick-starts the brain into clear thinking by taking it away from the situation that required an angry response. Try listing the ingredients in a favourite recipe or the films of a specific Hollywood film star; or if you too have completed The Knowledge, recite the route from Charing Cross to London Zoo.*

- *Sometimes it helps to move way from the situation; take a short walk or even go and sit in the toilet for a few minutes.*

- *Always practice deep breathing.*

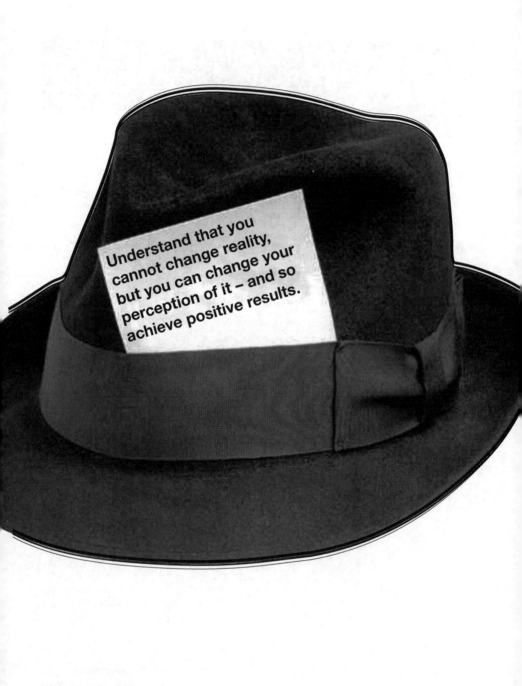

Chapter 4

Change your mindset

After leaving Soho, Ferdi picked up three grungy looking teenage girls headed for Euston station. They told Ferdi they were in a band called Do Not Bend and were taking the train to Manchester to play a 'gig' in a pub. Ferdi said that in his day, bands went on tour in decrepit transit vans; the Do Not Bend girls said they preferred to let the train take the strain so that they would arrive relaxed and, as they put it, 'ready to rock'. Instead of a tip, they gave Ferdi a signed copy of their Compact Disc. He did not mind because, if they made it big, it would be worth a fortune on eBay. It pays to be an optimist Ferdi, he said to himself as he tucked the CD into his glove compartment.

It was nearly lunchtime and Ferdi fancied Chinese food. He was heading to his favourite, the Hot Wok, when a couple of twenty-somethings hailed the cab. Ferdi knew that most cabbies on their way to lunch would have ignored them and stepped on the gas, not him though. 'A fare is a fare,' Ferdi would say to the other cabbies who often went on to moan about the lack of work or how much takings had dropped since the recession. Ferdi pulled over and the man and woman got in.

'Cable Street please,' said the man, 'and we've got an important meeting, so as fast as you can.'

'No problem,' Ferdi replied and then added, 'lovely weather we're having, isn't it; do you think it is going to snow?'

'Why are taxi drivers obsessed with the weather?' The woman said with more than a hint of sarcasm. Ferdi wondered what made her react in that way. Most probably she was concerned about her meeting, he thought. He pulled away from the kerb and set about getting to Cable Street as quickly as possible; after all, the faster he got there the sooner he could have his lunch. Ferdi happily ran through the Hot Wok's menu in his mind, trying to decide what to have with their world-famous crispy duck.

The man was in his early 20s and the woman appeared a few years older, both were smartly dressed and well groomed. After staring out of the windows in silence for a few moments, they forgot about Ferdi and began chatting to each other. 'I hate working for Cathy!' said the woman. Her arms were folded and she was wearing a frown; she did not appear to be looking forward to the meeting they were heading towards.

'Really!' replied the man, 'I quite like her.'

'Well, you haven't been working for her as long as I have.'

'True,' was his reply, and clearly thinking the matter closed, added, 'shall we go through the pitch again?'

'No, I can't be bothered, we'll be fine.'

'This is my first pitch and I want to get it right,' he said passionately, 'and it is a really important account, it will be great for the company if we win it.'

'But we've been through the pitch about twenty times already and anyway, it can't be that important or Cathy wouldn't have sent the new boy.'

Ferdi could not help overhear their conversation and was curious why the woman had such a negative attitude to her job and her colleague. Ferdi glanced at the man in his rear view mirror; he wondered how he might react. He now had his arms folded as well; he did not look very happy either.

'Look, Sarah,' he said, 'if we do not get this right, it will affect the whole office. Perhaps I should do the pitch myself and you can go back to work and explain to Cathy why you couldn't be bothered.' Good for you, thought Ferdi.

He might only be the new boy but he was prepared to stand up for what he believed was right.

'Paul! Remember, you are only the graduate trainee, you're not actually an account executive and you don't know enough to do the pitch by yourself,' she said sarcastically. 'Anyway, I didn't realise you and Cathy were such good friends.'

'We are not "such good friends" but Cathy's my boss and I think she is okay,' he said and added, 'why do you dislike her so much anyway?'

'She's a liar,' Sarah replied, still staring out of the window with her arms folded.

'A liar?' he repeated, thinking he might be about to discover some interesting office gossip. 'Really? What did she lie about?'

'What didn't she lie about?' was Sarah's reply.

'I don't know, tell me more,' he said, turning to face his colleague. Ferdi wondered what could have happened between Sarah and her boss to make her so miserable. Hearing about workplace situations like this made him even happier to be his own boss.

'At my interview, Cathy was full of how great this job would be and all the glamorous things I would get to do. She even said there was the opportunity to travel.'

'Oh!' Paul said. He sounded disappointed. 'Is that all? I am sure you will get to travel, eventually. You've just got to put in the work.'

What Paul was saying made sense to Ferdi, but Sarah's body language showed that she was far from convinced.

'She shouldn't say that someone will be going on trips to Paris, if they won't,' Sarah moaned. 'Cathy made all these promises so I'd want the job and then didn't deliver. It's just not fair.' Ferdi glanced at the man in the mirror, intrigued as to what he would say next and how he might react to his colleague's negative attitude. Paul did not bother to reply.

Both passengers went back to staring out of their windows in silence. The traffic around the East End of London can get ridiculously busy between midday and 2 pm, but, being a London Taxi driver, Ferdi knew the best routes and they had managed to avoid any serious hold ups. He hoped his passengers would be pleased that they were making such good time.

'How much longer, mate?' the man asked Ferdi.

'About five minutes or so, nearly there,' was Ferdi's reply and then added, 'do you mind me asking what line of business you're in?'

'Public relations,' Paul replied.

'Public relations,' Ferdi said, 'that sounds interesting.'

'Might sound interesting, but it's mostly pretty boring,' said the woman.

Ferdi laughed and said 'You must have been in the job a long time.'

'About 12 months but it feels like forever.' Sarah was still staring out of the window as she answered. She did not want to engage with Ferdi, but the cabby was determined to find out more.

'So why did you take a job that was so dull?' he asked.

'On paper it was my dream job but it turns out that all I do is write press releases and talk to journalists on the phone. Not quite what I expected.'

'What did you think you'd be doing?' he asked, genuinely interested. He had never met a 'PR' before. The closest he had ever been to one was Samantha Jones in Sex and The City, Marina's favourite TV show.

'I thought I would be jetting off to meet clients in Paris and New York, stuff like that,' she muttered. Even she did not sound convinced once she said the words out loud. Her colleague raised his eyes in disbelief.

'But no-one can do that all the time, can they?' asked Ferdi. Then he turned his attention to Paul, 'Do you feel the same way about your job?' he asked.

'No. Not at all,' was his immediate reply. 'I only finished University this year and I feel lucky to have got on to such a great graduate training programme.'

'Do you think you'll stay with the company when you've finished the graduate programme?' asked Ferdi.

'I really hope so, it is such a good opportunity,' he said with natural enthusiasm. 'It is a small company but it is going places. I hope they keep me on.'

'I can see why you were sent on this pitch,' said Ferdi, ' you have got a great attitude and it will get you through most things; even the boring bits of your job. Because, let's be honest, every job has its boring bits, even mine.'

'Surely not,' Paul said with a smile, 'a cabby's life must be full of excitement and glamour.'

Ferdi laughed, 'I love my job but sitting in a queue at Paddington or cruising the streets looking for a fare certainly is not glamorous. There's nothing wrong with the boring bits of a job, it's what you do with them that counts.'

'That sounds ominous,' said Paul. 'I'm scared to ask what you do to jazz up the dull bits of your day.'

'Don't worry,' replied Ferdi, 'I don't get up to anything dodgy. I do all sorts, really; I try to keep my brain sharp with mental exercises, sometimes I'll take a short break in order to clear my head, but mostly I accept that the quiet or boring times are just part of my job. It's all about your state of mind.' Sarah raised her eyes towards the ceiling; she clearly thought Ferdi was talking nonsense. Paul, however, did not. 'I think you're right,' he said. He then took a deep breath, turned to Sarah and said, 'Do you think it might be your attitude to your job that is making you miserable, rather than the job itself? Loads of people would love to be an account executive.'

Sarah looked shocked. She could not believe that Paul, the 'graduate trainee' had the audacity to suggest she had the wrong attitude to work. Ferdi smiled to himself; he liked Paul more and more.

'There's nothing wrong with my attitude,' she answered in a voice full of indignation. Ferdi thought it might be a good idea to diffuse the situation and try to improve Sarah's mood. If things continued like this between them, the pitch would go badly wrong.

'I bet lots of people applied for your job, didn't they?' he asked Sarah.

'Yes,' she said quietly, ' more than two hundred, apparently.'

'They must have really liked you at the interview, then,' Ferdi said, hoping to cheer her up a little.

'I suppose so,' Sarah replied. She still looked unhappy but Ferdi was determined to change her frame of mind for the better.

'What was it about you that stood out from the other 199 or so applicants?' asked Ferdi. Sarah thought for a second or two and Paul turned to face her. He was as interested as Ferdi to hear how she had got her job. It was something he had often wondered about back at the office.

'Cathy interviewed me, she said she liked my enthusiasm and that the test press releases I'd written were some of the best she'd ever read.' For the first time the woman smiled; the memory of the interview had finally lifted her spirits.

'You must have been delighted when she told you that,' Ferdi said, feeling relieved that they had hit upon a subject that she enjoyed talking about.

'I was over the moon, actually,' she said, 'it really was brilliant.'

'That alone probably wasn't enough though. Can you remember how you sold yourself to your future boss?'

'I said that I'd be enthusiastic, that I'd learn from her and work very hard until I made it to the top.'

'And what's the top?' asked Ferdi.

'Trips abroad, meetings with the clients; that sort of stuff.'

'I see,' said Ferdi, 'so do you think that if you did what you said you would do in your interview, you might get where you want to be; i.e. Paris and New York?'

'I do work hard,' she said begrudgingly, 'but I suppose you might have a point.'

'You've obviously got all the skills you need to be one of the best in the business,' said Ferdi. 'If you combine that with a positive attitude and resilient mindset, nothing will be able to stop you.'

'No matter how good someone is at their job, if they are miserable all the time or their attitude stinks, they won't last long,' said Paul, being careful to talk generally rather than about Sarah in particular.

He is very resourceful and thoughtful, said Ferdi to himself, he will go a long way in whatever career he chooses.

'I had this bloke in the back of my cab the other day,' said Ferdi. 'All he did was complain about his job. Turns out he works in a call centre for a company that sells printer cartridges or something like that and you'd never believe it but he said he hates selling and hates talking to people on the phone. So all the things he does not like about his job are his job. I told him that there is no point in complaining about having to do the things that you are paid to do,' laughed Ferdi. 'People are peculiar.'

'It is okay for you to take a break or do mental exercises when you're bored, but I can't do that,' said Sarah. So, she had been paying attention earlier, thought Ferdi.

'I know it is different when you work in an office, but the answer might be to view the parts of your job that you do not like, differently. Rather than pick up the phone to a journalist thinking that you are going to have a horrible or boring experience, see it as a crucial part of your job and future success and choose to do it to the best of your ability,' said Ferdi passionately. He knew from experience that a negative attitude could hold you back in life, as well as your career.

'Next you're going to tell me that people know if you're smiling when you talk to them on the phone,' she said with a hint of a smile.

'They do!' exclaimed Paul and Ferdi in unison just as the cab pulled up at Cable Street.

'Thank you,' said Sarah as she got out of the cab, 'you have made me think about my attitude to work.'

'People think it takes a huge amount of work to change how they think, but thoughts are one of the very few things we can change instantly. It might need practice to make positive thinking a new habit,' said Ferdi, 'but trust me, it is worth it in the end.'

'I'll keep focused,' she replied.

'If you find yourself slipping, try taking a short walk, even around the office, or smile. You'll be amazed at how much better it will make you feel.' Sarah grinned at him and got out of the cab.

Ferdi pulled away and headed for the Hot Wok; nothing was going to get in the way of his crispy duck this time.

FERDI'S THOUGHTS

"No matter how good someone is at their job, if they are miserable all the time or their attitude stinks, they won't last long."

"Does my job ever get me down? No job is perfect and each has its own difficulties and frustrations; it is how you deal with them that matters."

- Believe that you are as much in control of your attitude to work, as you are your day-to-day emotions.

- Make an active decision to tackle the less exciting aspects of your work with the same enthusiasm as you do the parts you enjoy – at the very worst, it means you will get through those tasks quickly and then move on to the enjoyable parts.

- Changing your mindset is possible anywhere, even in the office and there are many tricks you can try. For example:

  - *Change your posture – sit up straight and avoid slouching.*

  - *Move around - take a short break away from your desk, even if it is only for a few minutes.*

  - *Use focused thought; try listing everything you like or even love about your job.*

  - *Remind yourself why you go to work every day; whether it is to pay the bills, go on holiday, support your family or maintain your self-esteem.*

Avoid projecting your
problems into the future:
In the end all things pass.

Chapter 5

Seeing the Positives Vs Negatives

What Ferdi would have liked to do after his lunch of crispy duck and steamed prawn dumplings, was get his head down and have a quick nap. However there were still a few hours of work to be done so he thought he would try the taxi rank at nearby Waterloo Station. He counted thirty taxis waiting to reach 'point', so he decided to drive around the station to see if he could find a fare near the London Eye or Parliament Square. Point is what London Taxi drivers call being at the front of the queue at a rank. Once you reach 'point' you should take the customer at the front of the queue wherever they want to go.

Ferdi was heading along York Road towards Westminster Bridge, when he spotted a businessman pulling a small case on wheels. As Ferdi drew near, the man put out his arm and called out, 'Taxi!'

'It's all about the timing,' he said happily to himself as he pulled the taxi over.

'Heathrow airport, please,' said the fare. A flyer, Ferdi could not help smiling. His day just got better and better. A flyer is a fare that takes a taxi to the airport and all cabbies love them. 'Yes sir,' answered Ferdi. Heathrow was his favourite flyer and would mean a fare of between £40 and £75, depending on the traffic and terminal. In addition, if Ferdi managed to get to the airport quickly and without any hiccups, there was always the possibility of a handsome tip. Ferdi pulled away from the kerb and headed west.

'Which terminal are you flying from?' Ferdi asked.

'Four, please,' said his passenger as he pulled out some documents and started reading. The fare looked busy so Ferdi left him to his work and pondered which route to take.

Ferdi crossed Southwark Bridge and hoped that the traffic would be light along the Embankment. The river was his favourite part of the city and he tried to travel along it as often as possible. Today was proving to be a special day and, as if to highlight this, he hit green light after green light all the way. His cab sailed past Battersea Bridge, along Cheyne Walk and up to the Kings Road. They caught their first red light at the Earl's Court crossing; Ferdi was beaming.

'I don't suppose that happens every day,' said the fare. Ferdi was surprised. He had thought his passenger was engrossed in paperwork and assumed that he alone had enjoyed the magical green run.

'Whoever decides the traffic-light phasing makes sure it does not. But that's politics for you,' said Ferdi with a smile. 'You're not a politician, are you?'

'Worse than that, I'm afraid,' he answered, smiling back at Ferdi's reflection in the rear-view mirror, 'I'm a banker.'

'Didn't think there were many of you left,' laughed Ferdi and added.

'Seriously though, how is the world of banking these days?'

'Things are slowly getting back to how they should be, but it isn't easy. The problems we face now have as much to do with people as finance, I am afraid.'

As always, the traffic on the Talgarth Road was backed up through the lights, so Ferdi had a chance to observe the person sitting behind him. In his rear-view mirror, he saw a man in his mid-40s, balding, wearing a bespoke suit and what looked like designer spectacles. He seems like a nice enough bloke, thought Ferdi as the lights turned green and the line of traffic slowly moved forward. Ferdi's concentration returned to the job in hand — getting the passenger to Heathrow. They were on the elevated section of the A4 before the banker spoke again.

'The public blame the banks for everything bad that is happening in the economy,' he said with a heavy sigh.

'The headlines in the press suggested that a lot of the problems were caused by banks,' responded Ferdi.

'True. Nevertheless, it is not all our fault. Anyway, banks are full of people and a lot of those people have lost their jobs too,' he said sadly.
'Yes and I've heard all about those golden handshakes.' laughed Ferdi. 'I wouldn't mind losing my job if I was in line for one of those.'

'Very few staff got big pay-offs; most of those who have lost their jobs are ordinary people like you and me, they might have got a couple of months' wages but that is it. It is interesting though, because a lot of the problems now are with the people who are left behind, those still working in the industry.'

'How so?' asked Ferdi. 'Surely having a job in this climate is something to be grateful for.' Ferdi was surprised that anyone would be unhappy about having a job, especially a good one in the City.

'The people who kept their jobs have a deep sense of resentment because they are doing more work for less money in a sector that is widely despised. While in their eyes, those that were made redundant got the big pay-offs and probably a brighter future.'

'If they managed to get another job.'

'Yes, and it's a big "if". However, sadly, most of my staff do not think that way,' answered the banker. That is because we humans have an in-built

tendency to focus on the negative rather than the positive, thought Ferdi.

'What about you?' he asked his passenger. 'How do you feel about being a banker?' Ferdi was interested in how he felt about being one of those left behind.

'Me? I have a very different perspective to most of my colleagues. I give thanks every day that I still have this job. I get to keep a roof over my head and to feed my family. I will do everything I can to make it work,' he said with real feeling, 'I wish I could pass my enthusiasm for the job and the future on to my team and my boss.'

'Have you tried?' asked Ferdi. He was impressed that even when surrounded by so much unhappiness, this man was still able to be enthusiastic about his work. It must take a huge effort on his part but one he clearly thought worthwhile.

'I wouldn't know how,' replied the banker.

Ferdi turned into the Terminal 4 passenger drop-off point. They had arrived at the airport in good time but Ferdi did not want the conversation with his fare to end; there was something important that he wanted to say. The banker pulled out his wallet to pay but, before he could get out of the cab, Ferdi said, 'I don't know much about the world of banking but I've learnt a lot about people by driving this taxi. Many of us get stuck in a bubble of misery that is entirely of our own creation. Sometimes, hearing another person talk with the passion, enthusiasm and also common sense you did just now, can be enough to burst that bubble.'

'It is not very British, though, is it,' replied the banker, 'all this showing emotion and sharing of feelings. I'm not sure if I can do it.'

'A stiff upper lip will not get you anywhere in this life but showing you are human might. There's nothing wrong with sharing your emotions if they are good ones and positivity and enthusiasm are about as good as it gets,' replied Ferdi, 'and you've got plenty of both. Anyway, what is the worst that can happen?' laughed Ferdi. 'They run to HR to complain that their boss is trying to encourage and motivate them.'

'My goodness,' said the banker warmly, 'a motivational black-cab driver, I didn't know such a thing existed.'

'Sometimes I even surprise myself,' said Ferdi with a smile, 'but I have learnt through experience; talking about how you feel and maintaining a positive state of mind makes life better for everyone.

'True,' said the banker. 'You've given me plenty to think about.'

'Enjoy the rest of your day,' added Ferdi. At that, the banker headed off for his flight, but not before thanking Ferdi for a fast and inspirational journey and handing over a crisp, new £20 note as a tip. There was definitely something special in the air, and it did not feel like snow.

With a big smile on his face, Ferdi headed to the Terminal 4 rank. Perhaps he would reach point just as a plane load of Japanese tourists passed through the automatic doors. Today, anything was possible.

There were six cabs in front of Ferdi at the Terminal 4 rank. Not too bad, he thought as he waited to reach point. Ferdi had his fingers crossed that the passenger he picked up would be a friendly tourist looking for a ride into the centre of the city, rather than a short hop to another terminal or one of the airport hotels. He watched businessmen, tourists and aircrew get into the cabs in front of him and wondered who he would get. When he reached point, a well dressed, elderly man with a small suitcase and a walking stick got into the back of his cab. Ferdi waited for him to settle into his seat before pulling away. The fare wanted to go to West Kilburn. That will do nicely, thought Ferdi with a smile.

"There's nothing wrong
with sharing your emotions
if they are good ones."

"Do I ever tire of sharing my 'keep calm and carry on' ethos with my passengers? Never. It is what makes me the man I am. Taking a little time to make others feel happier has to be a good thing and it is guaranteed to make me feel happier too. Anyone can do it, whatever their job."

• *Share your passion and enthusiasm with colleagues; some of it will rub off.*

• *Try not to make assumptions about colleagues, take time to listen to them and find out what is causing their problems and concerns at work. As a result, you will be in a much better position to help change their mindset.*

• *Accept that it is better to be labelled as someone who tries always to look for the positives at work rather than being labelled as having a 'can't do' attitude.*

Recognise when you are distorting thoughts. Step back and think of a more balanced response instead.

Chapter 6

Being in Total Control

Ferdi was sitting in a cafe enjoying a nice cup of tea and chocolate brownie with friend and fellow cabby Chris when the snow that had been promised all day, finally began to fall.

'Snow, that's all I need,' grumbled Chris. Chris had only been on the job for two hours and was hoping to have a high-earning night shift.

'Don't worry, Chris,' said Ferdi, 'I'm sure it won't snow for long and look on the bright side; it is freezing, people will be fighting over cabs tonight.'

'Not with my luck,' answered Chris, 'I'll end up snowed in somewhere with a drunken banker in the back.'

'Come on, mate,' Ferdi laughed, 'think positively. I'm sure you will have a great shift, and don't be rude about bankers, I met a really great one today.'

'Yeah, right!' Chris moaned. 'I'm getting back on the road, might be some bread and butter work out there somewhere. Do you need a hand to your cab, it looks slippery?'

'You probably need a hand more than me,' laughed Ferdi. 'My cab is right outside.'

'Oh yes,' replied Chris, 'I forgot about you and your parking privileges; get home safely.' And with that, he rushed off into the night.

'Have a good night, Chris,' Ferdi called after him, smiling to himself.

55

Chris always made him laugh.

Chris was one of Ferdi's closest friends and they had done The Knowledge together, riding around on their mopeds in all weathers trying to learn the runs. Chris got his badge after just three years. It took Ferdi another twelve months to get his and become a Licensed London Taxi driver. The two friends met up for a chat over a cup of tea as often as their shifts and fares would allow.

The snow was falling heavily by the time Ferdi got outside. I might as well stop for the night, he thought. Why get stuck in a snowstorm when I could be at home warming myself in front of the fire. He was just getting into the cab when a well-dressed man in his fifties called, 'Taxi!'

'I'm just about to call it a night, mate,' Ferdi replied, as the man slid across the snowy pavement towards him.

'Please take us home,' he pleaded, 'my wife has a terrible headache and can't face the underground; we'll give you a really good tip.'

'Where are you going?' Ferdi asked.

'Finchley. Please!' Ferdi would have preferred to go straight home but Finchley was not too far out of his way and he could imagine how difficult a journey on the underground could be in this weather. And, he thought, a big tip would be the perfect way to end the day.

'Okay, it's almost on my way,' answered Ferdi. 'Where's this wife of yours, then?'

With that the man's wife appeared, teetering along the slippery pavement in a pair of very high heels. Her husband held the door open and followed her into the back of the cab.

'12 Avenue Road, Finchley,' she barked crossly.

'No problem,' answered Ferdi as he pulled away from the kerb and into the slow moving traffic. He put her demeanor down to her headache and decided to get them home as smoothly as possible.

The couple made small talk in the back of the cab and Ferdi listened to a weather report on the radio. He tuned in just as the Met Office gave out a severe weather warning; heavy snow was expected overnight. Oh dear, Chris would not be happy. I hope a half-cut banker has not hailed him, smiled Ferdi to himself.

'The roads will be slippery so I'd recommend you wear your seat belts.' Ferdi advised his passengers.

'Okay, thanks,' replied the man. However, neither of them strapped themselves in, instead they sat in silence staring out of their respective windows. Ferdi was concentrating on the traffic and did not think about his passengers again until he heard the man speak. 'How much did you leave for a tip?' he asked his wife.

'I didn't leave anything, the service was terrible,' she hissed. Ferdi sensed that the woman's headache was the symptom of a larger problem rather than the cause of her bad mood. He knew that in these conditions, his focus had to be on his driving and thought it was probably best not to get involved.

'It wasn't terrible, I think they were just short staffed,' her husband replied.

'Too bad! Anyway, a tip is a reflection of service. There was no service; ergo, no tip.'

'Of course there was service, we ate, didn't we?' The man's tone of voice changed as his emotion moved from one of frustration to anger.

Oh dear, thought Ferdi, it would probably be in the man's best interests to drop the subject until his wife was in a better mood. If they carried on like

this, they would end up in the divorce courts.

He was beginning to wish that he had not agreed to give the couple a lift home. However, he reminded himself, he had picked them up and now his job was to get them to Finchley safely. Ferdi closed the partition between him and his passengers, hoping it would cut out some of the bickering from the back.

'It would have been preferable if we had not gone out for dinner.' His wife reacted angrily with her voice raised, 'I could be at home relaxing in the warm, instead of being stuck in this bloody cab with you.'

Her headache is going to get a lot worse unless she calms down, Ferdi thought and, for a moment, he considered giving her some tips on deep breathing, but it was only for a moment; he instinctively knew that any attempt to help would inflame the situation more. This couple's problems could only be resolved if they talked openly about their feelings and emotions and were prepared to listen to what their partner had to say. It would take a lot more time than a taxi ride to Finchley would allow, even in the snow.

'It was your idea to take me out to dinner, so that we could "clear the air". Fat lot of use that was, it has just reminded me of all the things wrong with this marriage,' the husband said with contempt.

'Don't you dare talk to me like that!' shouted the wife at her husband who looked shocked at her violent reaction.

Great, thought Ferdi, full-on domestic meltdown, just what I need in a blizzard. He could not help wondering who would be paying the fare; he hoped it would be the husband or else he could probably say good-bye to his 'really good' tip. Ferdi smiled to himself, oh well; you can't win them all, he thought and turned off the main road hoping that taking a short cut through Mayfair would mean avoiding the worst of the traffic.

'All I said was that you should have left a tip,' her husband sounded defeated and probably wished they had stayed home as well.

'Shut up!' she screeched, 'just shut up! I can't stand to hear your voice anymore.'

This is going to be an interesting job, thought Ferdi as he glanced at his passengers in his rear-view mirror. It was quiet now and each was sitting at opposite ends of the seat looking out of the side windows. Both had their arms and legs folded and were facing away from each other, not the body language of a couple madly in love. Ferdi decided to keep his head down and get them home as fast as the weather would allow.

The snowfall was even heavier now and the huge flakes had already started to settle on the pavements and roads. The streets looked beautiful and people were throwing snowballs and attempting to build snowmen. Nevertheless, as pretty as the snow was, Ferdi knew that if it continued to fall like this, the roads would be gridlocked in no time.

Ferdi's phone rang; it was Chris. 'Bloody snow,' Chris exclaimed, 'I am calling it a night and heading home. You home yet, Ferdi?'

'Not yet,' Ferdi whispered, 'picked up a couple of fares wanting to go to Finchley. They're arguing in the back and I'm going to get stuck in the snow at this rate.'

'That's what you get for being greedy,' Chris laughed 'you should have gone straight home.'

'Thanks Chris, very funny.' smiled Ferdi.

'See you tomorrow, Ferdi.'

'See you Chris. Good luck.' Ferdi hung up the phone and glanced at his passengers. As he did, the husband pulled out an iPod, selected a track, closed his eyes and sat back in his seat.

Good idea, mate, Ferdi thought, listen to some music, it will help your brain go into a more relaxed state. He hoped that the wife would do the same, and then all he would have to worry about was the weather, the traffic and the state of the roads.

In all his years as a cab driver, Ferdi had never encountered snow like this. Cars were skidding as they braked and people were slipping and sliding on the pavement. At the moment, most of the pedestrians looked happy as they marvelled at the unusual weather but, if it continued to fall like this, chaos would follow; this city's streets were not made for snow.

Ahead of Ferdi, brake lights came on and the row of traffic came to a sudden halt. Ferdi gently squeezed his brakes, he did not want to skid into the car in front, and he was very aware that his passengers were not wearing seat belts.

Ferdi was craning his neck to see what was causing the hold-up when he heard a loud tapping on the glass partition between him and his passengers.

He turned to see the wife on the edge of her seat and slid open the partition.

'What's the hold up?' she asked, abruptly.

I am not sure,' he replied cheerfully, hoping that his positive demeanor might influence her own. 'It's probably just the weight of traffic.'

'Can't you turn around and go a different way? I want to get home now.'

Ferdi looked at the solid traffic behind him and the parked cars at either side. 'I don't think that's possible as this is a one-way street,' he answered slowly and calmly, 'but once this traffic moves forward I'll be able to take a right turn.'

She sat back in her seat and pulled out one of her husband's iPod ear buds.

'Why did you hail a cab? We would have been home by now if we'd taken the underground.' Her husband had been relaxing and took a second to realise what he was being berated for.

'You had a headache. I thought a cab ride would have been more comfortable and soothing,' he replied sarcastically, 'I got that wrong, didn't I!'

The traffic showed no sign of moving and horns were being pressed; the euphoria at the snow had passed and drivers were becoming irate. Ferdi took a deep breath and slowly exhaled. He was determined to remain in a calm state.

Just as he completed his exhalation, the phone rang; it was Marina.

'Hi love, are you all right?' he asked.

'Yes, I am fine, but the snow is bad here. How are you?'

'It is bad here too. I am stuck in Mayfair and the traffic is not going anywhere. I don't know what time I'll get back.'
'Are you on your way home now?'

'No, I've got a fare to drop in Finchley, then I'll be on my way.'

'All right, I will put your dinner in the oven. Drive carefully and get home safely.'

'I will. Thanks, love and I'll see you later.'

He ended the call just as the wife's knuckles rapped on the partition once again. 'Yes, madam,' he said as politely as he could manage.

'What the hell is going on? What are you doing talking on the phone when you're supposed to be getting us home?' Ferdi felt himself getting

angry with his passenger and paused before he answered. He did not want to be sarcastic or rude, as it would not help the situation. Instead, he told himself that her headache, her bad mood and negative state were a result of the problems in her marriage and the weather; none of it was his fault.

Ferdi glanced at his Keep Calm & Carry On postcard and was just about to answer when he spotted a traffic warden working his way up the row of cars talking to the drivers one by one. 'I'm not sure what's happening,' he said with a smile, 'but I'll ask this warden, he might know something.'

As the traffic warden drew close, Ferdi opened his window, 'What's happening, mate?' he asked.

'There has been a traffic accident and the road is blocked. Because of the snow, the tow truck cannot get here. It's going to be a while.'

'Can anything be done to move the cars behind us, then we might be able to reverse out?' Ferdi asked hopefully.

'I'll see what I can do, I can't promise anything though.'

'Thanks, mate,' sighed Ferdi, grateful that someone was willing to do something helpful. And a traffic warden! Who would have thought it?

'So what's happening?' asked his passenger.

'It looks like we are going to be here for a while. You might want to consider getting out and taking the tube,' Ferdi suggested. It probably would be a quicker journey for them and it would mean that as soon as he got out of this jam, he could head for home. The woman prodded her husband in the chest.

'We haven't moved for ages, and now the cab driver is telling us to get out and take the tube!' she said angrily.

'There is a traffic accident up ahead and a row of cars behind us so there's nowhere I can go. I just think it might be quicker for you on the underground,' interjected Ferdi. He did not want the man turning on him as well.

'Yep, I think you might be right,' he said, where's the nearest station?'

'Green Park is five minutes away and Hyde Park about ten; it might take a little longer in the snow.'

'I don't believe this!' the wife exclaimed. 'Cab drivers are supposed to know the best routes; why did you bring us down this narrow one-way street when it is snowing? Any idiot would know that's a really stupid thing to do.'

The temptation to respond in the same rude manner was strong, but Ferdi realised that in this situation the only thing he had total control of was himself. He could not affect the weather, the woman's emotional state or the traffic but he was determined to keep his state of mind positive and calm. Ferdi glanced at his Keep Calm & Carry On postcard and smiled to himself. It really helped him to have it there as a constant reminder. There are occasions when frustration or anger can be useful states, but this was not one of them.

Ferdi closed his eyes and took a deep breath, then happy that he was in control of his emotions, turned to the woman and said, 'Unfortunately I could not foresee the traffic accident. This would have been a good route if it had not happened. Would you like to stay in the cab and hope the traffic clears soon or pay your fare and walk to the tube?'

'To be honest, darling, I think we're wasting money and time sitting here,' said her husband warmly. 'Lets walk to the tube, it will be quicker.'

'Oh no! I can't walk in the snow in these shoes,' she wailed.

'Don't worry; I will help you. It might be fun and I will buy you some new shoes to make up for everything,' he replied and gave her a hug. Ferdi

smiled to himself; now that he and the weather were the common enemy, their relationship had improved considerably.

'I'll pay for the cab,' stated the man firmly. Ferdi's ears pricked up; maybe he would still be in line for a tip.

'Don't tip him,' responded his wife. 'He shouldn't have taken this ridiculous route; a better driver would have had us home by now.'

'Of course not, darling,' the man answered. True to his word, he paid the fare and asked for the change. It is definitely time to go home, thought Ferdi. I think my luck just ran out.

No sooner had his passengers got out of the cab, than the traffic began to flow. The warring couple stood and stared in disbelief as Ferdi pulled away. He watched them turn and start their walk to the underground station.

Ferdi began the long slow drive home. The amount of snow had clearly caught the local authorities by surprise and the roads had not yet been gritted. Luckily Ferdi knew the route home like the back of his hand and careful driving got him there in a little over an hour.

As Ferdi pulled into his drive, Marina came out of the door wearing her winter coat and walking boots. 'Where are you off to, love,' he called out. 'It is not really the sort of weather for going for a walk.'

'Very funny,' Marina replied, 'now let me help you out of the cab, the path is very slippery.'

'Thanks Marina,' Ferdi replied, it has been a long day.' Marina and Ferdi slowly made their way into the house and closed the front door.

FERDI'S THOUGHTS

"There are occasions
when frustration or anger
can be useful states."

"Do some passengers push me to the limits of my patience? Yes, but I will always do everything in my power to stop other people's negative states taking over my emotions. How? Read on."

- *Ask yourself – If I am not in control of my emotions, who or what is? Do I want to give away control of how I feel to someone or something else?*

- *Do not allow other people to take control of you by letting their rude behaviour, bad moods or negative attitude affect your own.*

- *Instead, ask yourself why they might be behaving this way.*

- *Finally, take yourself away from the situation by using deep breathing or focused thought.*

Chapter 7

Home Truths

Ferdi would smile when people told him that his positive attitude must have been something he was born with. They would often then say to him 'I can't change - it's just the way I am!'...

The day that Ferdi got his licence to be an All London Taxi Driver was amongst the happiest of his life. It had taken him four years to learn the 320 runs, as the routes are called that fall within six miles of Charing Cross.

He was on his way home and looking forward to celebrating in the pub with his friends that evening, when the driver of a soft drink delivery lorry swerved to avoid a cyclist. The driver lost control of his vehicle, which then mounted the pavement and trapped Ferdi under its front wheels.

Much, much later Ferdi would joke that he did not know what had hit him. In reality, the first he knew about the accident was when he woke up three days later in the intensive care unit of St Thomas' hospital. Marina was at his side when he woke and he could tell she had been crying but he had yet to discover why.

Marina told him a lorry had hit him while he was walking along the pavement near the Strand and that his legs had been damaged. Marina asked a nurse to call Mr. Parkinson, his surgeon, to clarify exactly what had happened since she did not know how to tell him herself. 'Surgeon,' Ferdi whispered to Marina after the nurse left, 'he sounds important.' 'He is,' Marina replied softly, 'he saved your life.'

Mr. Parkinson explained to Ferdi that after the accident, he had spent eight hours in the operating theatre and although the surgical team had managed to save his life, they had not been able to save his legs. Both of Ferdi's legs had been crushed under the lorry's wheels and the damage to his bones and the surrounding tissue was so extensive that amputation below the knee was the only option open to them.

Ferdi listened to the surgeon but did not say a word. The medication he was on made his brain feel fuzzy, so Ferdi struggled to take everything in, but he understood enough to know he would never be able to walk again and he would never get to drive a London Taxi. He hoped he was dreaming but deep down inside he knew he was not; Ferdi was in so much pain that what the surgeon was saying just had to be true. Marina's heart broke as she watched the tears roll down his cheeks.

Ferdi did not speak to anyone for the next five days. Marina, Chris, the doctors and nurses all tried to get him to talk about how he was feeling but he could not and would not. Ferdi did not want to speak because the only thing he wanted to say was that he would rather have died. He wished that the surgical team had not wasted those eight hours on saving his life.

Six days after the accident Ferdi woke up in the side ward he had been moved to and realised his right ankle was itching. He started to laugh and called out for a nurse, they must have made a mistake, his legs were still there and he could feel them. The nurse gently explained that what he was feeling were phantom pains where the nerves that served his legs continue to communicate with his brain. No one can quite explain why it happens but 80% of amputees suffer from phantom pains at some point or other. The nurse pulled back the bed covers to show Ferdi what was left of his legs. Marina insisted that she heard his scream in the cafeteria where she was buying a cup of tea.

Ferdi came home from hospital in a wheelchair; everyone was there to greet him, but Ferdi was not in the mood to celebrate and asked to go straight to bed. The last thing he wanted was to talk about how he felt or what he would do next. He did not have a brave face to put on. Marina sent their friends and neighbours home and asked them to give Ferdi time, but she knew he had fallen into a deep depression and had no idea how to get him out of it.

Nothing Marina could do lifted Ferdi's spirits. He only left the house for hospital visits and would not see anyone or talk on the phone to any of his friends or relatives. Ferdi's specialist explained to Marina that he was grieving for his past life and that the depression would pass in time. 'And if it doesn't?' Marina asked. 'Then we'll get him psychological help,' replied the doctor. As the days turned into weeks, Ferdi spent his time sitting in the wheelchair watching television. Marina did not know what to do to get her husband back; she no longer knew the sad, quiet man she was sharing a house with.

From Ferdi's point of view his life was as good as over. He knew he should be grateful to be alive but wasn't. 'Look on the bright side,' Marina said to him countless times every day, 'at least you're still alive.' However, Ferdi could not see a bright side; he was surrounded only by darkness and despair.

It was his GP, Doctor Juttla, who recommended that he try prosthetic limbs. It had been suggested at the hospital but Ferdi insisted that he would not have 'peg legs', as he put it. If he could not have his own legs, he did not want any at all. Marina suggested that he was cutting off his nose to spite his face, but the hospital said not to push him into it. He would come round to the idea in his own time.

Doctor Juttla explained that the rehabilitation would be difficult and that he would have to learn to balance and to walk all over again, 'but,' she said, 'being able to walk will give you back some day-to-day independence and, if all goes well, in time you might be able to drive.' Ferdi said he did not

care about walking, driving or balancing. He was perfectly happy to stay at home for the rest of his life, but Marina made the appointment at the clinic anyway. At his first appointment, Ferdi had a rigid dressing applied to his legs and later that week attended his first fitness session; building up his muscles would take time. Once the first prosthetics had been fitted, Ferdi set about learning to walk again. To say he was unenthusiastic would be an understatement but his physical therapist, Nicola, would not give up on him and ultimately, it was her enthusiasm and commitment that started the process of giving Ferdi his life back.

Nicola suggested that Ferdi contact the Limbless Association's Volunteer Visitor Scheme because meeting someone who had been through a similar experience might help him come to terms with what had happened. 'Great,' Ferdi said, 'that will be lovely. We can both sit around moaning about how terrible our lives are and comparing stumps.' Marina took the number and arranged for a volunteer to come over to the house. Ferdi did not know the volunteer was coming until he walked into the room.

Joe was thirty-five and he had lost both his legs in a car accident two years previously. On Joe's first visit, Ferdi did not say a word; he and Joe sat in silence drinking tea. After an hour Joe said, 'I'll be off now, Ferdi, I have got to go and pick my girlfriend up from work. I'll see you next week.' Ferdi complained to Marina that he did not want tea and sympathy from a complete stranger just because he had no legs, but she simply ignored him.

The following week Joe returned. Marina made the two men a cup of tea and left them to it. Joe did not pressurise Ferdi to talk; instead they sat drinking tea and watching Countdown. When it was time for Joe to go, Ferdi asked, 'Are you coming back next week?' 'Same place, same time,' replied Joe with a smile, 'and I'll bring you a present.' Ferdi found himself counting the days until Joe returned. He did not know why as they had barely spoken a word to each other.

When Joe arrived he handed Ferdi a box. 'That's for you,' he said. I hope you like it.' Ferdi opened the package and inside was a coffee cup. Printed on it was the phrase 'Keep Calm & Carry On' and a small crown. 'Thanks,' said Ferdi sarcastically, 'Just what my life is missing, another coffee cup. I do more than sit around drinking tea and coffee, you know.'

'Good,' replied Joe. Now, would you like to hear how I got my life back together?'

'Not really,' replied Ferdi, 'but I suppose you're going to tell me anyway.'

'I am,' said Joe, and he did. Joe explained that like Ferdi, the first he knew about losing his legs was upon waking up in intensive care and, like Ferdi, he felt despair, frustration, and anger at what had happened to him. However, unlike Ferdi he had decided that although he could not change what had happened, he would not let it ruin the rest of his life. Within three months of his amputation, Joe was learning to walk with the aid of 2 sticks and now, two years on, he drove his own car. 'But, it was not easy,' Joe explained, 'learning to live without legs was one step forward and two steps back.'

'Is that supposed to be a joke?' Ferdi asked, 'because it isn't very funny.'

Joe became Ferdi's good friend and life teacher. He taught him how to smile and then laugh, he taught him how to reframe his negative thoughts and instead look for the positives in everything. He took him to the pub and the park and gradually reintroduced Ferdi to the world.

However, the biggest lesson that Joe taught Ferdi, through all the dark moments and the pain and struggle was that he, Ferdi, was the one in control of how he felt and therefore how he lived the rest of his life. It was a lesson that he had to remind himself of, time and time again, but one Ferdi was determined not to forget.

Eighteen months after the accident Ferdi had his driving ability checked and re-took his DSA taxi driving test. He passed.

Two weeks later, he collected his disability modified London Taxi and took to the road. Seventy-four weeks, two days and eighteen hours after passing The Knowledge and losing his legs, Ferdi picked up his first fare as a licensed London Taxi driver.

Further Information

If you would like further information on how to
Keep Calm and Carry On
we offer the following services based around the
message of Keep Calm and Carry On:

Workshops
Seminars
Keynote speeches
One to one coaching
Leadership development programmes
Team building

Visit our website for details:

www.KeepCalmAndCarryOnTraining.com